M000240015

POETRY

—— *of a* ——

KING

POETRY

of a

KING

REV. DAMON GREER

Charleston, SC
www.PalmettoPublishing.com

Poetry of a King

Copyright © 2021 by Damon Greer

All rights reserved
No portion of this book may be reproduced, stored in a retrieval system, or transmitted in any form by any means–electronic, mechanical, photocopy, recording, or other–except for brief quotations in printed reviews, without prior permission of the author.

First Edition

Paperback ISBN: 978-1-63837-374-2
eBook ISBN: 978-1-63837-375-9

This collection of creative works was spiritually written with the Holy Spirit as my guide. They were meant to motivate, uplift and encourage those who are believers. To walk closer with the Lord, and to remain anchored in Christ. To remind ourselves who is at the head of our lives, and being dependent upon Him. These inspirations are meant for us to go the extra mile and walk righteously before Him.

Let us Pray: Father God in Heaven please forgive me of my sins, and created in me a clean heart. Renew a right spirit in me right now Lord. Let your presence have your way in these creative works. Father I pray that this collection of spirit filled displays will bless someone. To bring them back on the path, to remind them that Greater that is He that is in me, than he that is in the world. Father I know that I am simply a vessel that needs your daily nourishment, who craves your love in my life. May blessings fall upon all who partake of these spiritual works. Amen.

St. Augustine once said: "Thou hast made us for thyself, and our hearts are restless until they find their rest in thee. Whoever does not want to fear, let him probe his inner most self. Do not just touch the surface, go down into yourselves; reach into the farthest corner of your heart."

Saint Anselm The Father of Scholasticism
Once said, oh "Lord my God, teach my heart where and how to seek thee, where and how to find thee. For I do not seek to understand in order to believe, but I believe in order to understand."

Read these spiritual works with great conviction and watch how the spirit moves in your life.

Even in our most tumultuous times. He is our very source of strength in our time of need. A very present help in our time of danger.

THE RAINY SEASON

The rain just keeps falling in my life, the storms are a constant, the storm clouds just keep harboring over my life. But I will not wilt to the storms. I will not allow the storm clouds to get me down. As the rain falls and the floods pour into my life. Still I will maintain the course. Jesus is the way. Let me not veer left, or right. My direction has been set, my course has been predestined and it remains Christ. So God lift me over my storm clouds and reveal to me my destiny.

The rainy season represents our problems and issues and conflicts and heart ache and pain and through it all, God is able to do exceedingly abundantly above all others. I will not succumb to my disappointments and fears and issues and problems, but stand on the strong foundation of the Lord. The rainy season is but for a moment, but God's word is forever. When the hurricane force winds blow into my life causing major damage, I will look towards the hills which comes my help. I will not allow temporary setbacks to become permanent solutions in my life and still I will stand. Lord God you are my rock, and my foundation that I hold on to. So when the rainy season comes, let me be reminded that God is my rock and foundation.

Blessings…

FAILURE IS NOT AN OPTION

Although I've failed many times, I keep getting up, never giving in. Although I've fallen many times and my knees have suffered great damage, I stay confident that my Lord and Savior is with me. Failure is not a option. Satan you have no place here. The windows are shut, the doors are locked and my heart is fixed on the Lord. Failure is not an option. Often my path gets obscured , but you Lord are a light on the path. Reminding me that my direction must be you God. Failure cannot reside here, because I'm protected by your strong hands.

DESTINY

My destiny is at hand, my future is before me. I've come this far by faith, and im not looking back now. Mission accomplished in phase 1. Ok, but now it's time to go further, now it's time to elevate , next phase of life, no time to relax, no time to smell my own Rose's. My destiny is at hand and I'm determined to blaze the path that's set before me. I'm in a fight of my life, and I can't stop now, I won't stop now. Decision's, Decision's, Decision's, my destiny is before me. Life presents so many twist and turns. So many obstacles. Which way will I go? Which way will I fall? I only know one way, and that way is up. I only know one path and that's with my Lord and Savior. He's already told me all things are possible through Him. He's already told me , I can look to the hills which comes my help. He already told me, He is the way, the truth and the light. My journey has prepared me for this moment at hand. I'm in a fight of my life and my destiny is at hand. Devil get thee behind me. You cannot have my future, you cannot have my happiness, you will not steal my destiny, you shall not prevail , you will not win, because I've already won, I'm already victorious. Jesus assures me of that. So I'm putting the evil one on notice, with all his plots and schemes. You can't win, because I'm not alone, I travel with King Jesus. I cannot lose with the stuff I use.

I'm ready to spread my wings and soar above my storms that's coming my way. Because Jesus Christ shows me the way.

FADING TO STRENGTH

Fading in and out of conscienceness, wishing that the pain would go away. Hoping for the best, expecting the least. My mind playing tricks on me. My focus fades, my concentration is broken. I'm looking for relief in all the wrong places. As my eyes close to a flutter, all I see is colors, black, white, green, yellow I'm lost in a sea of despair, drowning in my disgust. Jesus is my answer, let us run with vigor and determination with a renewed confidence. He straightens My path and gives me strength. He sees my struggles and provides me with the comfort of a king. I am a King. Yes , a King, mighty and strong, despite my troubles, God has His Hand on me. Thankful, humbled and Blessed.

WORTH IT

As I ponder my thoughts and survey my steps, I can't help but to wonder is it worth it? Am I wasting my time? What is the benefit?

What's in it for me? The world has beaten me up, and knocked me in the dirt. My life has been full of detours and one way streets. Is it worth it? The Potholes of life have Tragically pestered and upset my flow. Is it worth it? I have been through the storms and hurricane force winds. I've been in the hail storms of life and survived the constant attacks of the Satan. Still is it worth it? Yes, I was beautifully built by God, just for this. I was God made and built to last. Built with a purpose. I was carefully and skillfully design by the greatest architect of our time. The creator and orchestrator of life. The one that gives life, the one that nourishes life and the one that is life. When I think about His goodness and what He has already done for me. It is a constant reminder of How He continues to keep me, even when I truly don't deserve it. How His blood was shed just for me, how he leads me and guides me over the terrains of life. Yes its worth it. He walks with me and talks with me. Its worth it. When I step off into the fiery furnace, He's with me. When I swim in the deep waters of life, He's with me. He is my life preserver. He is my strength when I'm weak, He is my guide when I'm lost. He is my pulse that gives me life. Yes its worth it. Never let the rainstorms of life to cause you to give up. God is the way the truth and the light.

Blessings…

5

HEY

Hey I'm watching you, yeah you, I'm waiting on you to let me in. Open your heart to me so I can run roughshod over your life. Hey you, are you listening, I know you can hear me. Open your heart to my darkness and I will give you nothing but broken promises, empty unfulfilled dreams and pain like you never seen before. Hey can you hear me now, I am the prince of darkness, I stand for no other reason but to destroy you. To devour you. To steal your joy ,kill your peace and snatch away your happiness. Do you know who I am, yes! but I also know who my Father is. He is strong and mighty, the King of Kings, the prince of peace, our strong tower, I will never let you in, I will never follow your path. God has predestined my path, He already showed me I am a true heir to The King. So hey, get thee behind me Satan, you and your Imps are merely distractions and not permanent fixtures in my life. I know where my help is, I know that my strength is in the Lord. So hey ,move on Satan there is no food here for you, keep it moving.

Blessings...

DEMONS

Demons are always eager to ensnare, trap and seize the lost. We must stay on the Holy ones path to unlock the grips of Satan on our destiny. When he attempts to choke us into submission with his deadly attacks, we must stand strong, declaring God's truths. Holding on to God's truth and professing God's truths. Demons look to feed off those who are weak spiritually and have no direction, no path and no light. Let us be champions of the light, constantly drinking from the fresh spring waters of the Lord. Trusting and believing that God is the bread of life and those that believe will never hunger. Demons have no strength over Authentic believers, they stand on the foundation in spite of.

STILL DREAMING

As I sit and ponder my thoughts, and search the depths of my heart. Still Im dreaming, dreaming of a day when all men have been truly created equal. Still dreaming , dreaming of discrimination that clutches our hearts, fades away like the early morning fog. Still dreaming ,where freedom is not just a word but a movement that is displayed in our actions. Yes, I'm still dreaming, hoping that my walk is equal and worthy to the next persons. Still dreaming, dreaming of a day when we all can truly get along. Yes I'm dreaming, dreaming that one day, one day, that the hate that exist in our fellow man, dissipates as we participate in love for all. Still Dreaming, that one day, gun violence is silenced by the will of the Father, who commands us to love one another as He has loved us. Yes I'm still dreaming of that day when we all can walk side by side, hand in hand for one common cause and then I woke up.

Blessings...

LOST

Lately I've been losing myself deep in my thoughts confused and wondering about, fluttering in and out of reality. What's real and what's not. What's good and what's not. My direction is obscured the path appears block, my mind is cluttered often time I'm confused by all the noise, all the hatred and hopelessness that's on the surface. But you God is a constant and my anchor. You Father I lean on and depend on. I get my comfort in you. I realize I was once lost but now I am found. Found because of your righteousness, found because your foundation never gets over run with the rigors of life. I know that I am safe in your hands, secure in your safety net. Lost in your beauty and amaze by your goodness. If I'm lost, I'm lost in your willingness to love me anyway in spite of my imperfections. In spite of my back sliding mentality. Yes I'm lost in the fact that you are who you say you are. Thank you Lord for being the best of me.

SEEKING YOU

As the fog gathers before me, my vision gets obscured by life's circumstances, but I'm still seeking you. The wind often blows me off the path and takes me on the life of detours, but its you oh Lord that I'm seeking. My mind often wonders and drifts back and forth from the darkness to your magnificent light. Questioning myself, pondering my thoughts, wondering what is it all about, but then a small voice leads me back to you. Yes I'm seeking you. There have been times I've lost my way, but you Lord give me strength, you are my anchor and my way maker. I'm seeking you, I know deep in my heart, I'm nothing without you. You are my hope that sits in my heart. Every breath that I take is because of you. Every step that I make is predicated on you. You are my faith that settles me when I'm lost in the dark. You give me that assurance, that all things are possible through you. So no matter what, I'll be seeking you.

TAKE OFF THE CHAINS

Take off the chains, I see on the Horizon, freedom. Freedom to be whatever I want to be, but the chains must fall. They will fall, my destiny is at hand, my future is at stake. I refuse to surrender to my naysayers, my opposition and doubters. God has a plan for me, destined for me, ordained just for me. So the chains must fall. Yes I see in the distance on the Horizon freedom, but its so far away, with Racism and prejudice standing in the way. I can't give up though or succumb to my fears, and challenges and disappointments and setbacks, and those who do not recognize me for me. I will not wilt to the judgement of others or negativity that proceeds from them, but stand anyway. The chains must fall. I will surge ahead, I will fight the good fight. The chains will fall and I will stand tall, because my strength is in the Father, and my faith is in Him. Victory is mind, so I will bust free, never giving up, never relinquishing my hope, my desire to live the bless life free as can be.

PEACE

In the mist of your pain is your peace.

The kind of peace that only I can give you. The peace that I give, I give in the abundance through me. A special peace, a long lasting peace. My peace is like no other in the world. So do not allow your heart to be troubled by the storms that may rage in and around your life. Stand firm upon my foundation. Lean not to your own understanding ,but in everything acknowledge Me. I am a constant and a anchor and a fixer of broken things. My peace surpasses all understanding, and I will guard your heart and your mind so fix your heart upon me and depend on me. Do not allow the wilds of the devil to disrupt and destroy your peace. Be reminded that I'm able to do exceedingly, abundantly above all others, so allow your peace to be in me and receive your crown for life.

Blessings…

SENT WITH A MISSION

I was sent to save you and give you abundant life. My mission could only be done by one, that's me. I was sent with a mission by my Father, to prosper you and not to harm you. I was sent, not to misinform you, but to conform you to the image of me. I was sent, not to frustrate you, but to comfort you. I was sent not to blind you but to enlighten you. I was sent, not to leave you guessing, but to show you things to come. I was sent, not to pull you down , but to build you up. I was sent, not to bring partial joy or peace, but to fill you to overflow. I was sent to feed you and not to starve you. I was sent to be example of agape Love. That's love base on the deliberate choice to love. I was sent to be your protector and Savior. Do you know me now? Do you recognize who I am. Will you come to me? I came for you.

Blessings...

CAN YOU SEE ME NOW

Can you see me now? I'm right here, can't you see me, I been here the whole time. I came so that you may have life and have life more abundantly. Why can't you see me, is it because you have allowed your worldly desires to over come my truths. Is it because you have ignored my spiritual teachings and preaching for a life of darkness. Can you see me? I've been here, you the one that left, you the one who chose death instead of life. Can you see me now. I'm the one who walked up that hill called Calvary and was nailed to a cross for all mankind. I'm the one who took on the sins of the world so you could not be dam to hell forever. I'm the one that loved you so much that I looked death in the face and then I defeated it for you. Do you know me now, can you see me now. I'm here to stay, and I will Never leave you or forsake you. Live like you know me.

Blessings...

MERCY

Have mercy upon us oh Lord. Mercy for our sinful ways, mercy for our disobedience, mercy Lord for walking in the dark places instead of walking in your amazing light. Have mercy upon us, we have been lost in all of our greed and misguided actions. Have mercy upon us Lord for our inability to walk on your path, turning our backs on your precepts and ordinances and decrees and commandments. We ask for mercy Lord because we have been lost, walking aimlessly in our worldly desires instead of staying on your foundation. We ask for your forgiveness and grace and mercy. Allow your incredible light to shine once again in our lives. No more do we want our way Lord. But yours. No more do we want to live in disconnect from you. You are our strength in a dry and thirsty land. You are our living spring water that replenishes us daily. Please Lord don't turn your back on us God, have mercy on us.

THE BEST OF ME IS YOU OH LORD

The Best of Me is You Oh Lord, The Best of me I adore, its the rest of me that I have trouble with at times. The more I try to live in your amazing Light ,the more the clouds of life attempt to damper that light. But you oh Lord, You are the best of Me. You are my Light, you are my direction, You are my shield and hope. You are my strength when I'm weak. You are my living bread and my fresh spring water. I know with you I will never thirst or be hungry. Thank You Father for being you, thank you Lord for being the best thing that has ever happen to Me. Yes you are the best of Me.

Blessings...

I'M IN A FIGHT OF MY LIFE.

Im in a fight of my life. Round 1I keep moving, staying on my toes,, trying to not get hit by the devils Haymakers. I'm in a fight for my life, I gotta keep moving, keep dodging these obstacles. Im in a fight of my life, realizing and understanding that my strength, my strength is in the Father, the one. He keeps me, He sustains me. He gives me the strength and the ability stand even when I'm being attacked by the wilds of the devil. Im in a fight of my life, trying to shake off these body blows and head shots. Got to fight back, got to utilize my secret weapon, got to use Gods word.. That same word that gives life, that same word that is life and that same word that nourishes life. Keep fighting, keep resisting, don't give up now. Stand firm and resist the evil one and he must flee. Stick and move, in and out, never giving Satan a easy target. Keep your head on a swivel never be surprised of the devils works. I'm in a fight of my life and the devil is trying to win. But I know that he cannot win, he will not win, because of who I serve. I may be in a fight of my life but I also know that the fix is in. I cannot lose. I will not lose. Because I know who's with me.

Blessings...

STILL I STAND

When the wind blows and storm clouds hang low, Still I must stand. When the fog impairs my vision, I will stand. The deep waters may rise in my life, and I'm choking on despair, but I will not allow the waters to overflow me. Still I will stand. I stand, I stand , I stand. When adversity taps me on my shoulder and slaps me in the face, I still must stand. When I fall on the jagged edge rocks, slipping, falling and it appears I can't get up, I will stand. I stand not because of me but because of what's in me. I stand because of God's strength that gives me perseverance, that gives me staying power. I will not quit, I will not surrender, because of He that is in me, stands with me.

Blessings…

BLACK RAIN

The rain is fallen ,fallen and falling some more. Storm clouds hanging over our heads. Black rain, poisoning our system, Polluting our veins, taking over our minds. Turning our hearts black, making us cold and numb, leading us down a path full of despair. Rain rain go away never coming back not one more day. Black rain leave us alone. You can no longer penetrate us and tempt us, you can no longer effect my family poisoning our brain and turn us against each other. Black rain the sun will shine again, the storm clouds will dissipate and the light will illuminate leaving it like it never happen.

RESIDUE BLESSINGS

Lord God I need you. Lord God I'm walking with you. Your word says if l come closer to you. You will come closer to me. Well Father, I'm determined to walk up close to you. So much so that I want to receive the residue blessings.

The residue blessings are those small blessings that we didn't even ask for but God seen fit to give them to us anyway. Residue Blessings are those blessings that God provides us when we overlook or failed to consult God about them and He provides them anyway.

That's just favor from the most high God. We must remember to walk close to Him and not only receive blessings but we will also get the residue blessings as well.

Blessings...

STAYING THE COURSE

As the storms rage in and out of my life like angry waves crashing against the banks of despair. Still I must stay the course. When my obstacles rush into my path, still I must stay the course. When my disappointments invade my personal space, I must stay the course. When trials come and tribulations fleetingly penetrate my life and attempt to rock my foundation, I will stay the course. Because my anchor is in Christ, my direction is Christ and despite what I may go through. I am reminded that the Lord is the way, the truth and the light. So the course has already been set and my objective is simple, follow Christ . The path has already been established through Jesus Christ, so dispite all of my circumstances, I know that my help cometh by the Lord.

Blessings....

NO MORE

As the storms rage in and out of my life, I peer into the mirror as to remind myself. No more will I allow lifes circumstances to win. No more will I live in 2nd and 3rd position when God has declared that I am a heir to His Kingdom and Royalty to the King. As I look deeper into the mirror and see the deep embedded scares that had been left by the struggles of life. I shake my head in disgust, reminded of the unfair treatment of my people. Get your knee off my neck, stop shooting us in the back, stop harassing us because of the color of our skin. Stop ignoring us in the job place. Give us our just do. No more will I succumb to my struggles, no more will I let the evil ones suppress and beat me like an old negro slave. Enough is enough, I'm busting free from my chains and escaping this nightmare. I picture myself climbing to the highest mountain top and screaming, let me be! let me be! I know my worth, I know my position. As the river crest and winds blow and the sun shines so ever bright, I will walk on this path, I will forever walk in His light.

Blessings...

SUSTAINABILITY

The driving force in me is you oh Lord. You are the light that fills my day, the light that encourages me everyday. It is your light that keeps me when I'm losing my way. You are my strength when I'm weak, you are the one that keeps me on my feet. When I'm down you will lift me. When I fall you will cushion the blow and pick me back up again. You are the one who keeps me when all appears lost. Yes Lord you are what sustains me. You keep me from losing sight of who I am. That reminds me that I am a King and a heir to the King of Kings. I am Royalty because of Jesus The Christ. I am above and not beneath. Yes you sustain me oh Father, even in darkness, it is your beacon light that shows me the way. You oh God, are my comforter and provider. You sustain me God, I will keep the faith regardless of my circumstances, regardless of my storms. My foundation is you, my strength is in you. You are my way maker. You are the one that I lean on. Please God continue to give me spiritual eyes to see that you are the one that sustains me.

Blessings...

I RATHER

I rather have Jesus in my life, yes Jesus. He is my Light that gives me direction. He is my Light that forever shines a Light on the path of righteousness. I rather have Jesus, the one that saved me. The one that gave me life. The one that gives Abundant life through Him. I rather live on His foundation, on the rock, where I know where my help is. Where I know where my peace is. I choose Him, because He is the way, the truth and the light. Yes I rather have Jesus, the one who walks with me , the one who talks to me. The one that continues to bless me in abundance.. The one who still covering multitude of my sins now and forever more.. Yes I rather have Jesus, the one who picks me up when I fall. The one who encourages me when I'm down. The one that strengthens me when I'm weak. The one who will shield me from the fiery darts. The one who says He is with me even in the deep waters. The one who says He is with me in the fiery furnace, that ensures me that He is a protector of the faithful. I rather have a sure thing a real thing. You decide.

Blessings...

RESTORE ME

Lord restore me, I've been through the fires and I've been through the floods, the rain just keeps falling but yet, I'm still here. The storm clouds are constantly hanging low and obscuring my vision. But you Lord are my anchor, you God are what sustains me. My hope is in you. My peace is in you. My joy is in you. Lord restore me. I'm searching for your comforting right hand which is strong and mighty. Hold me Lord, and don't let go. Keep me upright Father, because the devil is constantly on attack, seeking to destroy me. I know that I have drifted off the path and sunk into a cesspool full of sin. But I'm ready to come back home, repent and realign myself with you Lord. Yes restore me Father, renew my song and let it ring loud and clear. My desire remains you, your direction, your way. Here my cry oh Lord, and restore Me.

Blessings...

THE ESSENCE OF PEACE IS IN THE PRESENCE OF THE KING

The essence of peace is in the presence of the King. Many search far and near, looking for the elements of peace. Searching, yearning and desiring only what the Father can provide. Peace and harmony is not in our possessions, its not in our monetary gains. It's not in people, but in the King, The Father himself. The essence of peace is in the presence of the King. My focus , my desire is to draw closer to Him. To live my life in Him. Can you see it? It's ever so close, it's right before us. Will you find your peace or continue to walk in the storm clouds of life. Will you walk in it and bask in His glory. It can only be found In the confines of the Father. Its the kind of peace that fulfills the soul. The King of Peace that is in His hands, will you come into His presence? Will you run into His hands? The essence of peace is so sweet and dear, all we have to do is adhere to His plan and peace will be His brand, over our lives and in our soul. The essence of peace is in the presence of King. The path that I walk, I walk with great desire to draw closer to the Prince of Peace.

Blessings...

LOOK TOWARDS THE HILLS.

Look towards the hills which cometh my help. My help cometh from the Lord. The one that sustains me, the one that keeps me in perfect peace. I must look towards the hills, indicating and reminding myself, to keep my head up and my eyes set on Jesus, because my help comes from Him. He is my strength and my helper. When the tumultuous winds blow and the storm clouds draw near, my help is in the Lord. When despair and the rain falls, I will not turn from the Father, I will stay the course, I will stand in the rain. I will walk on the lighted path, regardless of my circumstances, regardless of my pain. I trust you oh God. Pull me out of the grips of Satan, tear me away from his plots and schemes and allow me to see your goodness even through all of the evil ones polluted attempts to snare me. You are my God, my comforter and provider. My faith will not waiver, or be moved by Satans attacks. I see the hills and God's amazing light, reminding me that I am not alone and victory is mind.

Blessings...

DANCING WITH THE DEVIL

The evil one is seeking whom he may devour. Seeking and peering through the window of opportunity that we give him. Searching for an opening, one little seam crack, one little sin that invites him in. Yes we are dancing with devil when we fall into deciet, and flirt with sin and walk off the path of righteousness. Dancing with the devil projects a slippery slope on a cliff that over hangs hell. Darkness is near and Satan is going about like a roaring Lion seeking his next dance partner his next victim. Will it be you, or you, or you. The lights flicker, the magnificent light is slowly fading, the path grows eerily small. We must stay focused on Gods goodness, and stay on the foundation in His light or you too will dance with the devil and fall into despair. We must decide, we must choose, you either all in with Christ or you not.

Blessings...

FREE

I'm free as I want to be, free as a bird, wings extended with the wind blowing in and out of my face. Soaring high above Satans tricks and schemes and plots and evil desires to have his way with me. I'm free, yes I'm free as I can be, living my life as a witness for thee. I know that the King is watching, and I am His witness. His witness indeed. I will not allow the devil to imprison me. To hold me hostage and take refuge in me. I will not allow the shackles of life to capture me, and beat me into submission. No I'm free, free as I want to be. I make this promise today, to remind me every time I find myself falling and drifting away from Him. That God has His hands on me. I must hold on, I must keep the faith. Because he has made me to be free, free as I want to be. My wings have not been clipped. My mind will not be altered, although I know that the obstacles of life will constantly come before me. I will not be deterred by the devils advances. I will not lay in the dirt, but fly like an eagle high above, wings extended, and mind focus. I'm free to experience God who is always with me.

Blessings...

TRIALS

The winds are blowing, and the trees are bending and the ocean waves are crashing against the rocks. It appears the storm clouds are hanging above my life and the dew is thick and the fog prevents me from seeing my way through. Even in the mist of all of this, you oh Lord are a beacon light for me. My trials may rage in my life, but you God are my strength, and my foundation. Please guide me Lord through the murky waters, pull me out of the quicksand and steady me God. It appears trouble is all around me, but you God are a fixer of broken things. A healer and comforter to those who need it. When my life appears to be falling out of control like a avalanche, you are my net that catches me and place my feet back on solid ground. Lord continue show me the way. Continue to lift me out of the dirt. Clean me up through your word and give me courage to stand in my storms. I must stand because I know that my help comes from you. I will not falter in my trails, but I will stay the course that has been set and ordained by you God. Show me the way, continue to shine your magnificent light on the path and I will never stop running this race that is before me. I will see my way through.

Blessings...

LORD HEAR MY CRIES

Lord hear my cries, as lay in the dirt, stuck in the mud, blinded by the darkness that surrounds me daily, wishing for one more chance, one more day, one more opportunity. Lord give me a chance, I know I've been lost in my sins, eating the nectar from the poison fruit, but please Lord hear my cries. The storms of life appears to have swallowed me whole. Devoured my testimony and led me into the wilderness. Lord hear my cries. I've turned from my evils ways, and looked into the depths of my soul, wishing for another chance, another opportunity, another day. Lord hear my cries. The fog is thick, the waters are murky and the fresh spring waters are nowhere to be seen. My hope is quickly fading in the distance and my faith is dancing on the edge of self-destruction. I look up to see a small glimmer of light, just enough to peer through the clouds, giving me a sign and then I woke up...

Blessings....

BLACK

As I sit and ponder my thoughts and look over my life. I gaze upon my flaws, my setbacks and troubles, and I see my journey. Hard but not impossible, tough but not unbearable, challenging but not unbeatable. My reflection in the mirror displays my black skin and lines of wisdom under my eyes and reminds me of my challenges ahead. When I look deeper in the mirror and look into my eyes, I see my torment, anguish and pain from all my disappointments and setbacks, and I am reminded that My fight is not over. I'm still fighting the good fight with all that is within me. I'm still fighting to be relevant, still fighting to have a say in today's world. Still fighting for equal rights, still fighting to live my life. Yes I'm black and proud of it. Black with all odds against me. Black with the same resistance from others not wanting me to succeed, but I won't give up, I won't give in. I have to stay encourage and remind myself daily that this too shall pass. When I turned from the mirror, I must never forget that God ordained me in my black skin to be what he has called me to be. A King who was chosen to live life in the greatness of the Father and reap the continuous blessings of Him in Him.

Blessings..

TWINKLE

You are the twinkle in my eyes. The bright and morning star. When I gaze upon you, I'm thankful for who you are. Oh so thankful for what you do and who you are in my life. That twinkle, that hope, that spark, that light that resonate in and around my life.You are the one, the only one who died so I could live the abundant life.You are my twinkle, when I think about your goodness and all that you do. It sends my heart into a frenzy for you. When the turbulent winds blow and the sand appears to make every step unsure, but then I look to you Lord. You are my foundation that stables me, my rock that protects me, my keeper who keeps me. You are my twinkle that moves the needle in my life. Oh I'm so thankful for you. That you came like no other and did what no others could do. I continuously look to you God, you are my strength, and my help. When I find myself losing my focus, and veering off the path, it's you I look to. You will forever be that twinkle in my eyes.

Blessings...

SEEKING YOU

I'm seeking you Lord, with all that is within me. The road gets obscured, my vision gets altered by the rigors of life, but I'm still seeking you. You are my constant and my rock, I yearn for you. My desire has not wavered my love has not faltered. I keep my mind stayed on You. Walk with me in the rain and I will bask in your magnificent light. When the elements of life have left me in despair and exhausted. I will stay on your foundation, and walk in your light and be an example of your light. I live because you live in me. My desires and hope is in you. My trust and faith is in you. I know I can't do nothing without you. You are my heart beat, my pulse, the very breath that I breathe is because of you. I will forever be seeking you...

Blessings....

THE MONSTER IN ME

My blood boils and rage has often consumed me. That monster is in me, and part of me is being fed by the devils hand. I fight daily to keep my sanity, to keep my faith, but that monster keeps calling me and calling me and calling me. His temptation has been set before me like a nice juicy steak and My appetite to live in the flesh, is truly at stake. He's attempting to drive me further and further into his darkness, until I'm lost. So many problems, so many issues, the edge of the cliff is in full view. That monster is in me. Satan the evil one, has me in his grips. That monster won't let me go, he got is claws deeply embedded into what I stand for. I'm in a fight, a fight for my flesh. But little does he know, God says He is with me, and that He will never leave me or forsake me. Yes that monster is big, but my God is bigger. He quenches my thirst, feeds my will, strengthens my soul and helps me to overcome the monster that is in me. The monster retreats and is beaten back by the Holy Spirit. Get thee behind me Satan, you monster, you evil one. God says you will not prevail over the righteous, you will not eat up my flesh. Suddenly I regain my strength, my footing and my hope. I'm reminded that you must have faith. Faith to conquer all demons, all powers and principalities. Yes that monster goes about like a roaring Lion seeking whom he can devour. But my Father in Heaven tells me to fight the good fight until death and receive the crown of life.

Blessings...

DELIVER ME

Lord deliver me, I've been walking for some time, on borrow time. Deliver me, suddenly I can't see, the fog is thick and I think I'm losing my mind. Delivery me, Father I'm walking aimlessly, like a sleep walker, please deliver me. The devil got his hands on my throat, and is choking the life out of me, deliver me. I keep slipping in and out conscious and the devil keeps pressing me, delivery me. I'm afraid I've lost my way, Lord deliver me. The storms are raging in my life like a water fall. Deliver me, I know that I can't give up, I can't give in, because with you Lord, I know that I win. Have mercy on me, and deliver me. I know that my strength comes from you, my hope is you, my direction must be you. Oh Lord, deliver me. My path is cluttered with so much debri, and so many obstacles. Please, please Lord deliver me. Suddenly I'm feeling my strength, realizing where my help comes from. Deliver me, as the tears flow and my heart opens and turns back to you, deliver me. Thank you Father, you been so good to me. I found renewed strength and a vigor to continue this fight in this thing called life.

Thank you Lord for delivering me.

Blessings...

CPSIA information can be obtained
at www.ICGtesting.com
Printed in the USA
BVHW022124081121
621087BV00016B/7